ISBN 978-0-331-38677-6
PIBN 11116242

WAR FOOD ADMINISTRATION
Office of Distribution
821 Market Street — Room 700
San Francisco, 3, California

Approx, 15 minutes
May 1, 1944
State and Area Supervisors
Can-Cut to fit allotted time

FOOD FIGHTS FOR FREEDOM — AT HOME AND ABROAD
(WRD WEEKLY SCRIPT #7)

Use of this weekly series has been cleared for time by the Office of War Information over the following radio stations: Z-Bar Network, Montana; KFBC, Cheyenne, Wyoming; KLO, Ogden, and KDYL, Salt Lake City, Utah; KTAR, Phoenix,
Arizona; Reno and Las Vegas, Nevada; KWG, Stockton, California; KXL, Portland;
KIDO, Boise, and KRLC, Lewiston, Idaho.

ANNOUNCER: Good _____, friends. What are you doing to help your country

              manage its food supply? What can you do? You'll find out if you

              listen each week to.....

              Food Fights for Freedom — at home and abroad!...a presentation

              of the Office of Distribution, War Food Administration.

              Today, _____ of the (state or area) office is going to give

              us more information about food. He'll talk about food for school

              children, first of all, then follow up with some late news flashes

              about food for homemakers, farmers and distributors.

              And _____, about this school lunch program.....I remember

              the government started it some years ago when it was distributing

              our big food surpluses where they would do the most good. But

              we surely don't have that kind of surplus any longer. What's

              the story on this War Food Administration program today?

OD: It's a war story, _____, about a wartime job that would need

              doing even if there never had been a peacetime school lunch program.

              To get right at a main reason for it, I think we'd all agree that

              there must be arrangements to give mid-day meals to children whose

              parents are in war industries. And those meals should be

              nutritious, too.

ANNOUNCER: There's no argument there, I'm sure....especially not from parents.

OD: No, it's the parents who most usually ask that a school lur

program be organized in their locality,....mothers who want 1

fill the need for women in industry, for instance....they car

go to work unless they're sure the children will be fed pro}

in their absence. Nowadays, if the mother is working,....ei1

at a paid or volunteer war job,...the children sometimes ha

be left with little or no supervision. And as far as the fo

picture goes, lunch is usually the meal that gets sacrificed

The working homemaker packs a cold lunch for her children o1

gives them directions to come home and take something from 1

icebox.

ANNOUNCER: That last would send the kids out on the streets at noon..

OD: Yes, and the same thing may happen when they are given mone}

lunch, if they have to buy food away from the school grounds

ANNOUNCER: Then -- maybe this is going too far -- but I should think ar

unsupervised lunch hour could be a factor in juvenile delin

and increase the possibility of accidents, too.

OD: You're absolutely right on both counts, according to educat

and juvenile authorities. So you can see why many communit

would be interested in a wartime school lunch program, even

other reasons. But those other reasons exist too, and the

one is Nutrition.

ANNOUNCER: Meaning that children should get the right food, along with

getting it in the right way.

OD: Yes -- the right kind of food,_____, properly prepared, at a reasonable cost. And school lunch programs can do all these things. You might not think cost was an important item these days when we hear so much about high wages, but it is. For instance the mothers living on the allotments of husbands in the armed forces. <u>They</u> have to watch their pennies, and so do many salaried workers and other people. A typical school lunch program, backed financially and otherwise by the WFA Office of Distribution and local sponsors, can provide children with a hot, nutritious meal for as little as ten or fifteen cents. Or even at <u>no</u> cost. The mass buying of food alone is a big cost-cutter that no housewife can equal.

ANNOUNCER: Good enough,_____. About nutrition itself, though.... you named that as a top consideration. How about some details....

OD: Well, take some of those families in war work. A housewife may not have enough <u>time</u> to prepare really nutritious breakfasts or dinners. So if a lunch is faulty too, the child may get two, or even <u>three</u> insufficient meals a day. In many cases lunch at school is the only hot and well-balanced meal a child gets.

ANNOUNCER: If that's the case, I suppose the Office of Distribution helps make sure that the school lunch is really a good one.

OD: Yes, we do, but I had better say right now that not <u>every</u> school lunch program is backed by the government. Many excellent programs operate independently, and have for a long time. When they <u>do</u> get financial support from our agency, though, they are expected to meet definite nutritional standards. Congress appropriates the money for this program, and it expects that money to do the greatest possible good.....

ANNOUNCER: So how do you make sure about it....?

OD: Our agreements with the school provide that each lunch will offer

from one-third to one-half of the child's daily food requirements

We designate two types of lunch according to the size of portion

served, and call them Type A and Type B. Both meals include meat

or a meat alternate such as eggs or dried beans,....and also a fru

vegetable, bread or cereal, butter and usually milk. The schools

receiving Federal aid can get up to nine cents per meal to defray

costs of a Type A lunch, and up to six cents for Type B.

ANNOUNCER: What about costs of labor and equipment needed to prepare lunches

Is that included?

OD: No, the Office of Distribution pays only for foods that are bough

from an approved list. Labor and equipment must be paid for by

the local sponsor....and the sponsor may be the Parent-Teachers

Association, some civic club, or the local school district. Spe

foods may be financed in the same way, or the expense can be met

charging the children a small extra fee.

ANNOUNCER: Then some school children are getting their lunches entirely fre

while others pay maybe a dime, or a little more....that is, in

programs sponsored by the WFA Office of Distribution. Am I righ

OD: Correct...

ANNOUNCER: And another question,.....about that "approved list" you mentio

What kind of foods are included in the list?

OD: The basic ones are milk and cheese, fresh and dried fruits, fresh
and processed vegetables, meat, poultry, eggs, butter, beans, peas,
and several others. But for less essential foods the list is
flexible. There's plenty of latitude for the school cooking staff
to serve a wide variety of well-balanced meals.

ANNOUNCER: Then the school takes responsibility for seeing that lunches
maintain high standards of nourishment.....

OD: Correct. However, our agency does have a good deal of literature
and poster material to offer,....there's a very fine pamphlet
suggesting nutritious and attractive menus used by many of the
schools. And all menus are based on the Basic Seven food chart
which we promote as a guide to good wartime eating habits. I
expect you've seen the chart.....

ANNOUNCER: I certainly have. It's practically a kitchen Bible nowadays.....
Well, _____, we seem to have covered the subject of Nutrition
pretty thoroughly. How about summing up the facts about this School
Lunch program before we go on to some news about food?

OD: All right....I'd say first that although these programs in many
cases started in peacetime, they are serving equally urgent needs
in time of war. Wherever we feed our children collectively at
school, we are helping to save food, labor and utilities.

ANNOUNCER: How about the health angle.....?

OD: The facts show that children at these schools are gaining weight
and tackling their studies with more energy. School principals
say that scholastic records have definitely improved, and attendance
records along with them.

ANNOUNCER: And about juvenile delinquency?

OD: The school lunch program has a marked beneficial effect, although no one would claim that it's a cure-all. By providing a place for children to stay and be well-fed at noon...under supervision of faculty personnel....we are taking one step towards defeating a juvenile problem much aggravated by the emotional stress of war.

ANNOUNCER: And finally, _____, I should think that the benefits to parents of these children.....particularly the working mothers....are one of the biggest features of the program.....

Now let's give our listeners some up-to-date facts from the food front. I'll help do some of the reporting, but you start us off....

OD: The regional Office of Distribution of the War Food Administration announces the release of small quantities of canned corn, orange juice, pumpkin and sauerkraut for civilian consumption. The releases cover supplies in excess of war needs, and the products will be resold to packers from whom they were originally purchased. Buell F. Maben, western regional director of food distribution, points out that War Food Administration resells to the trade from time to time as a result of changing war needs. The sales are generally small, and are handled in a manner which prevents disruption of regular markets.

ANNOUNCER: Civilians will be able to get better ice cream during May and June. That's because the permissible percentage of milk solids used in the manufacture of ice cream has been raised. And at least in cities with populations of 50,000 or more, people may get more, as well as better, ice cream. (MORE)

ANNOUNCER: This is because the quota of cream and milk products allowed
(cont.) dealers has been raised 25 percent for these same two months of the
flush milk production season. This definitely means more cream,
cottage cheese, buttermilk, flavored milk and milk by-products in
stock during the period.

OD: The WFA Office of Distribution says that prospective supplies of
early-crop onions are the largest in history, and at the same time
announces termination of shipping restrictions on remaining supplies
of the 1943 crop. Only a few hundred carloads of late 1943 onions
remain to be marketed. Thus restrictions in effect since last
August 30, which helped the armed forces and dehydrators to meet
their requirements, are no longer necessary. Under War Food Order
No. 77, the shipping permit plan now relaxed has been operating
in California, Washington, Oregon, Utah, Nevada and Idaho.

ANNOUNCER: Civilians will get fewer hen turkeys during the spring marketing
period. This is because the armed forces overseas are definitely
being given first chance. In War Food Order No. 97, effective April
21, the WFA Office of Distribution requires a set-aside of all hen
turkeys processed in sixteen turkey-producing states. These states
include California, Washington, Utah and Oregon. Until the armed
forces have been able to purchase 8,800,000 pounds of turkey, this
set aside applies to 100 percent of all birds processed. However,
the total number of turkeys wanted for the boys overseas is actually
only about half the number of hens usually marketed during the spring
quarter. These surplus marketings will be one source of supply for
civilians,/ after military orders are filled. In addition all producers who have less than 26 hens,
and who have no authorized processor within 100 miles, are allowed
to sell their birds for local consumption. When military quotas are
filled, the set-aside order will be suspended.

OD: Speaking of overseas requirements and their effect on civilian
        supplies, there's a good deal to say at this time about canned fruits
        and vegetables. The fact is, quantities of these foods available
        for civilian use from the 1944 pack will be drastically reduced.
        Here are some details.....

ANNOUNCER: From the 1944 pack, canners will be required to set aside for war
        needs a quantity of fruits and vegetables ranging from 26 percent
        to 150 percent of their average production in 1942 and 1943. This
        means, for example, that war needs will take about ten million cases
        of peaches. If the peach crop is not too good this year, civilians
        will find few canned peaches on their grocery shelves, or will have
        to pay more ration points to get those available. If the crop is
        a good one, and canners are able to handle it, ration points might
        even be reduced.

OD: The same reasoning, and approximately the same figures, apply to all
        other fruits and vegetables that go into cans, and which are needed
        in great quantities for shipment overseas to our fighters. Here's
        the list: Canned apples, applesauce, apricots, berries, cherries,
        figs, fruit cocktail, peaches, pears, pineapple, pineapple juice,
        asparagus, lima beans, snap beans, beets, carrots, corn, peas,
        pumpkin, spinach, tomatoes, tomato catsup, tomato puree and tomato
        paste. The set-aside on all these products averages well over 50
        percent of the average 1942-43 production period.

ANNOUNCER: In case the housewives listening in are downhearted about the canned
        fruit and vegetable situation after hearing these facts, here's a
        note of cheer.....they have the alternative of _frozen_ fruits and
        vegetables -- ration free, right now -- which make thoroughly
        acceptable substitutes for most of the canned products. (MORE)

ANNOUNCER: A lot of cold storage warehouse space is being cleared of these
(cont.)   frozen foods right now to make room for more critical items, and
there are bargains to be had on many of them.

OD: There will probably be a little more _meat_ for civilians this year
than in 1943 -- especially pork. In the case of beef there is
some uncertainty, and the answer will probably lie in how evenly
the marketing of beef cattle can be spread over spring, summer and
fall months. There is a natural tendency for cattle producers to
keep their stock on the range as long as possible, to take advantage
of the more plentiful and cheaper grass feed. But if too many cattle
are held on the range and then marketed all at once in the late
summer or early fall, the resulting "run" -- as it is called --
could very well swamp all slaughter facilities. To make a long and
complicated story short, orderly marketing should spread adequate
beef supplies evenly throughout the year. The alternate situation
would be likely to give us a beef surplus for a couple of months,
followed by a great shortage for many months afterward.

ANNOUNCER: Closing Remarks....

FOOD FIGHTS FOR FREEDOM -- AT HOME AND ABROAD
(MRD WEEKLY SCRIPT #8)

Use of this weekly series has been cleared for time by the Office of War Information over the following radio stations: Z-Bar Network, Montana; KFBC, Cheyenne, Wyoming; KLO, Ogden, and KDYL, Salt Lake City, Utah; KTAR, Phoenix, Arizona; Reno, and Las Vegas, Nevada; KWG, Stockton, California; KXL, Portland; KIDO, Boise; and KRLC, Lewiston, Idaho.

ANNOUNCER: Good _____, friends. What is this country doing to manage

               it's food supply...and what are you doing to help? What can you

               do? You'll find out if you listen each week to....

               Food Fights for Freedom -- at home and abroad!....a presentation

               of the Office of Distribution, War Food Administration.

               Today, _____, of the (state or area) office of this agency is

               going to give us more information about food....

OD: Yes,_____, and the information I'll start with this week

               comes from the War Food Administrator himself -- Marvin Jones.

               Mr. Jones has issued a general statement about our food supplies

               this year, and the prospects for 1945. I think everyone in the

               country will want to hear it.

ANNOUNCER: Ought to be very timely -- particularly with these new developments

               in rationing. So how does the overall food situation look to

               Marvin Jones and the War Food Administration -- pretty fair?

OD: I'll let the Administrator answer in his own words,_____. He

               says, and I quote: "Our food situation at this time is good, because

               farmers -- despite many wartime hardships -- have produced above

               schedule all along the line. Their remarkable job of hog production

               is one example. It has given us plenty of pork for our armed forces

               and fighting allies, while making possible the temporary removal

                                                         (MORE)

(CONT.)

the time being, suspended rationing on other meats, on all frozen fruits and vegetables, all dried fruits, lard, shortening, and most of the important canned vegetables. Ration points have also been <u>reduced</u> on many other items...."

ANNOUNCER: Then the American farmer is the man we all have to thank....

OD: Especially when we know, as Mr. Jones points out, that they have been handicapped by lack of machinery, and the loss of trained young workers to better-paid city jobs, or to the armed forces.

ANNOUNCER: I notice Mr. Jones uses such words as "for the time being"...and "our food situation <u>at this time</u>!...Does he mean things may not be so rosy later on?

OD: I'll quote him on that point too, because it's one of the main parts of his statement. The War Food Administrator says: "It must be pointed out that any food supply needs to be constantly replenished, because as soon as it's produced it starts being used up. Therefore having plenty <u>now</u> does not necessarily mean plenty <u>later</u>."

ANNOUNCER: How about some of these foods we seem to have so <u>much</u> of....like eggs, and cabbage, and potatoes....

OD: Mr. Jones mentions those too, and he explains that anything from weather to changing military requirements can transform a tempora abundance into a shortage. Or the change may be in the opposite direction, as it was with potatoes and onions.

ANNOUNCER: So all in all, we really can't have too much of any food nowadays...and a surplus is likely to be only temporary.

OD: That's it. After his statement about "having plenty now not meaning plenty later", Mr. Jones warns us that it will be even harder to meet out total food needs next year than in 1944. To quote him : "Spring planting has been delayed this year by unseasonable weather, and the feed situation is particularly threatening. Despite greatly increased production, and imports of all the feed our transportation facilities permitted, there is still not enough feed for the livestock we now have...."

ANNOUNCER: Does he suggest any remedy,_____or is there such a thing?

OD: Mr. Jones has a suggestion, all right, but I'm sure he wouldn't call it a remedy. What he has in mind is a plan to make the best of a bad situation, and prevent it from getting worse. Let me quote again: "Livestock and poultry numbers will have to be adjusted to the feed supplies we have available. This will require that we market throughout the year a greater number of hogs, cattle and poultry....that we cull our dairy herds to leave more feed for the best producers. Balancing of livestock and feed supplies will be in the interest of all consumers, and it will be in the interest of the livestock producers themselves... They are the only ones who can accomplish it..." That ends the quotation.

ANNOUNCER: It's a very interesting and significant statement, too. I
think it reminds us that we should be happy about this year's fine
food supply, and the recent rationing improvements, without being
blind to the possibility of harsher conditions later on. And I
guess that just amounts to saying that we still have a war to
fight. We still need to buy those no-point, low-point foods,...
plant Victory Gardens, and prevent food waste.,.,Now,_____.
we've talked about the food situation in general, so let's have
some news flashes about foods in particular.

OD: All right -- the first one ties in with that change on meat
rationing,...In fact it's an explanation of why the change took
place....

ANNOUNCER: Ought to interest homemakers,because I think the news caught most
of our "better-halves" by surprise,

OD: Well, the standard policy of the Office of Price Administration,
which of course works in harmony with the War Food Administration,
is to adjust point values to the prevailing supplies of each food.
If there's enough of a particular food, ration points may be
adjusted downward, or taken off entirely. One big reason for
taking most meats off rationing is the unpleasant one mentioned
by Marvin Jones -- that our feed supply is tight. And a reason
for lack of feed is the drought which has dried up range and
pasture lands in some of the producing areas. That's why there
has been extra heavy marketing of lambs, sheep and calves. Hogs
are also being marketed at a higher rate than usual for this time
of year.

ANNOUNCER: But what about those steaks and roasts? Why couldn't they be taken off rationing?

OD: Just because these particular cuts are not coming to market in big enough quantities. If the supply improves later on, we might get our T-bones without points too. But don't count on it,

ANNOUNCER: We can dream, can't we?...Okay, what's next in the news?

OD: The regional Office of Distribution has announced that butter manufacturers will be required to set aside 40 percent of their May production, and 50 percent in June. At the same time, civilian butter supplies will be slightly larger than during the first quarter of 1944....For a comparison of the two quarters, the butter allocated from April to June amounts to 432 million pounds, as against 410 million pounds available from January through March.

ANNOUNCER: How about the general picture? Will we have more butter during the whole year than we did in 1943?

OD: We will. Government war agencies will actually require less butter in 1944. About 17 percent of our annual production of creamery butter will go to the armed forces. Three percent will be purchased by the War Food Administration to fill for lend-lease, territorial and Red Cross allocations. The required set-aside right now is heavier than during the past few months, in line with War Food Administration policy of filling government needs during the months of heaviest production.

ANNOUNCER: I'll take the next item, _____. The regional WFA Office

of Distribution said today that government war needs will requi

the set-aside of 60 percent of all cheddar cheese manufactured

in May and June. Last year's set aside was 70 percent. Thus

civilians are now getting about ten million pounds per month

more cheese than at any time since last July....

OD: For more than a year, 25 varieties of fruits and berries have

been on a restricted list. They cannot be sold to wineries or

distilleries, except under certain conditions. This week a new

War Food Order -- or rather a new amendment to Order Number 69

withdraws two commodities from the restricted list. At the sam

time it prescribes new methods by which growers may request

permission to sell their crops for the making of products which

contain over 7 percent alcohol by volume,...that is, for the mak

of wines, cordials and similar products. The list of 25 fruit

and berries is now reduced to 23 by the withdrawal of elderberi

and cantaloupes. The remaining fruits and berries are; apple

apricots, cherries, currants, Concord grapes, dates, peaches,

pineapples, plums, prunes, blackberries, blueberries, Boysenbe

dewberries, gooseberries, huckleberries, Johnsonberries, Logan

Olympic berries, raspberries, Youngberries and strawberries.

ANNOUNCER: All of these products have prime importance as food, for milit

and civilian consumption. Therefore they must not be sold fo

the making of alcoholic beverages unless they definitely can n

be marketed as food. When they cannot be so marketed, specifi

lots of the fruits or berries may be authorized for sale to

wineries or distilleries.

OD: If you own fresh fruits or berries which you yourself have
        raised, you may appeal for release from restrictions to your
        County Triple-A Committee. You will not, as formerly, go to the
        County USDA War Board.

ANNOUNCER: If you are a processor, shipper, or anyone else who has acquired
        fruit from producers, and hold it in fresh, dried, juiced or
        otherwise processed form, you must request your release from
        "authorization officers" of the WFA Office of Distribution. The
        same procedure is required of wineries and distilleries which want
        to use restricted fruit. Field representatives of the Office of
        Distribution (including our present guest speaker Mr._____)
        have been designated as "authorization officers" in all major
        fruit producing areas..... What else do you have,_____?

OD: Well, we've just been talking about one of the 90-odd War Food
        Orders. We've mentioned them before under their old name of Food
        Distribution Orders. I'd like to say a little about how these
        vital wartime measures are made effective.

ANNOUNCER: How they're enforced, you mean?

OD: Yes and no,_____. Enforcement is part of the story, but
        it's the last part. Compliance with War Food Orders is a matter
        of voluntary cooperation between government and industry, more
        than anything else....

ANNOUNCER: And I take that to mean the teamwork has been good,....

OD: Outstandingly good. And I think the reason why there have been
        few prosecutions of food order violations is that these orders
        themselves are prepared cooperatively right at the start.

ANNOUNCER: You mean the various food trades have something to say about each War Food Order before it goes into effect....

OD: Exactly. Each trade is represented at Washington by a Food Trade Advisory Committee....and the committee is generally made up of members drawn from the national association of that trade — such as the National Cheese Institute or the American Meat Institute. These groups meet with corresponding branches of the War Food Administration to work out and discuss every War Food Order before it's adopted. From that point on, getting compliance with an order is mostly a matter of education.

ANNOUNCER: As an Area (State) Supervisor for the WFA Office of Distribution, you handle some of this education yourself, don't you? At least I've gathered that idea from conversations we've had before...

OD: You're right. All of our State and Area offices are responsible for helping local businessmen and food producers understand each War Food Order that affects them. Then they won't violate it through lack of knowledge. The Food Orders themselves are distributed very widely by Washington, and supplemental information goes to newspapers, radio stations, farm and trade papers, and individuals. But the Office of Distribution field men make a great many personal visits, too.

ANNOUNCER: That is, you drop in on a grocer or a baker and ask him whether he understands some War Food Order that applies to his particular trade....is that it?

QD: Correct. And if we happen to find that he has <u>not</u> understood
an order, so that he's making some infraction of the rules, we
set him <u>right</u> on it. This kind of spot check is being made
continually. We aren't trying to "catch" anybody violating an
order, but trying to help prevent mistakes from being made
inadvertently.

ANNOUNCER: Sounds fine to me,_____....but I imagine the cooperation
has to work both ways to be really successful. What I mean is,
the food trade people also have the responsibility of coming to
the Office of Distribution, if they don't think they understand
a War Food Order....

OD: You're right -- cooperation works double, and so far that's just
the way it <u>has</u> been working.

ANNOUNCER: On the other side, though, what happens if some firm wilfully
violates one of the food orders? Can it be prosecuted under law?

OD: Yes, if a thorough investigation shows deliberate violation, a
firm or individual can be prosecuted in court under the Second
War Powers Act. A case of this kind was filed the other day against
a paint manufacturer in Dallas, Texas. Government attorneys charge
the compnay with exceeding its 1943 quota of fats and oils allotted
for paint manufacture by 142,454 pounds. Then in California, a
short time ago, a baker and grocer were prosecuted jointly for
violating War Food Order Number One...that's known as the "bread
order". It prohibits consignment selling of baked goods, by which
a baking company delivers a grocer an excess of bread, and gives
rebates of some kind for the stale bread left over.

ANNOUNCER: I can see why the government might be tough about that kind of offense...the practice of overselling probably wastes a lot of good bread....

OD: More than you might guess,_____. I'll give you the figures — just to make it more clear why War Food Orders have to be written, and why they should be observed.

ANNOUNCER: Shoot!

OD: A survey was made of the results of bakery consignment selling during 1942. It was released by Secretary of Agriculture Claude Wickard to help explain the <u>need</u> for the "bread order". The figures showed that this peacetime practice caused the loss, throughout the nation in 1942, of 6 million pounds of sugar, 5½ million pounds of dried milk, and 4½ million pounds of shortening. These losses came either from an outright waste of food products, or from their diversion to animal feed.

ANNOUNCER: That's enough to convince me,_____. Thanks for coming over today.....

.....CLOSING REMARKS.

####

′ WAR FOOD ADMINISTRATION
Office of Distribution
821 Market Street, Room 700
San Francisco 3, California

Approx. 15 minutes
May 15, 1944
State and Area Supervisors
Can Cut to fit allotted time

FOOD FIGHTS FOR FREEDOM --- AT HOME AND ABROAD
(MRD WEEKLY SCRIPT #9)

Use of this weekly series has been cleared for time by the Office of War
Information over the following radio stations: Z-Bar Network, Montana; KFBC,
Cheyenne, Wyoming; KLO, Ogden, and KDYL, Salt Lake City, Utah; KTAR, Phoenix,
Arizona; Reno and Las Vegas, Nevada; KWG, Stockton, California; KXL, Portland;
KIDO, Boise; and KRLC, Lewiston, Idaho

NOTE TO STATE AND AREA SUPERVISORS: Suggest you time all scripts in advance.
News section of the script is a good place to make additions or deletions.
War Food Bulletins from this office are a good source of additional news items.

ANNOUNCER: Good _____ friends. What are you doing to help your

country manage its food supply? What can you do? You'll find

out if you listen each week to.....

Food Fights for Freedom --- at home and abroad!....a presentation

of the Office of Distribution, War Food Administration.

Today, _____, of the (state or area) office is going to

give more news of activities on the food front. _____,

what are we going to talk about this _____?

OD: First of all, our listeners ought to be very much interested

in news of the recently formed committees of business men in

(state) which will assist the War Food Administration to achieve

a more efficient food distribution.

ANNOUNCER: Food Distribution Advisory Committees.....

OD: Then there's the problem of the enormous amount of food that

we waste here in this country just in the normal course of

buying, storing, cooking and eating our daily fare. I have

some rather interesting dope on that.

ANNOUNCER: Food Waste in the Home.....

OD: And finally, there are some new developments on changes in th
             food picture.

ANNOUNCER: Okay. What'll we start with first?

OD: Well, I don't know whether or not your cigarette has tasted
             different lately, but I'm sure you've noticed that the ice
             cream you've bought, — that is, if you've been able to buy
             it, — in the last year or so hasn't had the same creamy
             texture, in most cases, that it used to.

ANNOUNCER: Yes, that's right, I have noticed that. And, as you imply,
             ice cream has been kind of hard to get. I suppose you can
             tell us why?

OD: The major reason is that war time demands on our production
             and supply of milk solids have been very great, and therefo
             the amount of milk solids going into frozen dairy products
             has been limited.

ANNOUNCER: Limited how? Do you mean limited by one of these War Food
             Orders you've told us about in previous broadcasts?

OD: That's right. One of the first orders that went into effec
             was War Food Order 8 on Frozen Dairy Foods. Beginning in
             February of last year, manufacturers of frozen dairy foods
             were limited to the use of 65% of the volume of milk solids
             they used during the base period — December of 41 to Decem
             of 42.

ANNOUNCER: That would account for the smaller amount of ice cream avai
             but how does that affect the quality?

OD: This War Food Order #8, among other things, also specified the amounts of certain ingredients that go into ice cream and other frozen dairy products. Specifically, it limited milk solids to 22% of the total ingredients. It however did <u>not</u> require mixing sherbets and ices with ice cream to stretch the supply of frozen dairy products.

ANNOUNCER: Well, so what? All I know about ice cream is that it's good to eat.

OD: The smoothness and creaminess of ice cream largely depends upon the amount of milk solids in it. That's not the whole story, of course, but that's the major consideration.

ANNOUNCER: I see. I assume that conservation of milk solids is important, or the order wouldn't have been issued....

OD: That's right....

ANNOUNCER: But just how much did it do? Has it really conserved any large amounts of milk solids for other purposes?

OD: This order is really important. And it's conserved a <u>very large</u> amount of milk solids for making butter and skim milk powder.

ANNOUNCER: Don't be coy. Tell us <u>how</u> much.

OD: We estimate that up to date, War Food Order #8 has conserved enough milk solids to make 125 MILLION pounds of butter and 55 MILLION pounds of skim milk powder.

ANNOUNCER: That's really amazing.

OD: When do I get my $64?

ANNOUNCER: You're on the wrong show, bud. Is War Food Order 8 going to continue in effect?

OD: Yes, it is, but with these changes for May and June, months of flush dairy production: the total amount of milk solids that manufacturers can use in the production of ice cream has been increased 10 percent over these months last year, and the maximum milk solids content of ice cream has been raised to 24 percent, up to 10 percent over what it's been till now.

ANNOUNCER: That means, then, that we can expect more ice cream for these two months, and richer ice cream as well.

OD: That's about it.

ANNOUNCER: Now, how about some information on these Food Distribution Advisory Committees you mentioned at the beginning of the program. Just what is a Food Distribution Advisory Committee?

OD: The name pretty well outlines the functions of the committee. They consult with and advise the War Food Administration on problems of food distribution.

ANNOUNCER: That sounds good, but its a little vague. Let's pin it down. Who serves on these committees?

OD: Representatives of the various parts of the food trade in the area in which the committee functions, such as representatives from bakers, wholesalers, retailers, meat packers, egg and poultry concerns, produce men, and so forth. An Office of Distribution Representative acts as chairman.

ANNOUNCER: In other words, it's what is called a <u>horizontal</u> committee.

OD: That's right -- we also have <u>vertical</u> sub-committees, composed

               of several representatives from one type of business -- such

               as the egg and poultry industry -- to take an example. This

               type of committee functions on a special problem or job peculiar

               to that one industry.

ANNOUNCER: I see. This type of committee works on things like the recent

               nation-wide drive to encourage greater consumption of fresh

               eggs that I've heard about.

OD: Precisely. The general committees worked in that, too, and

               the campaign is still going on in some places producing,

               incidentally, some surprising results. I hope to have a fuller

               report for you on that later in this series.

ANNOUNCER: Fine. Let's get back to the overall, or horizontal committees.

               What are their functions?

OD: Principally, three.

ANNOUNCER: And number one is....

OD: To advise the Office of Distribution through regular meetings

               of shortage and surplus conditions on all the foodstuffs they

               are concerned with in their regular business activities. To

               help us eliminate faulty distribution of these commodities,

               and to warn of impending shortages so there won't be maldistri-

               bution in the first place.

ANNOUNCER: And number two.....

OD: To evaluate and advise us of the effect changes in ration points are having on the movements of commodities at retail and wholesale levels. To recommend to us changes in ration point values in the light of their experience. These recommendations the Office of Distribution in turn passes along to OPA, which gives them serious consideration each month.

ANNOUNCER: Which brings us to the third job of Food Distribution Advisory Committees......

OD: And that is to assist the Office of Distribution to achieve and maintain compliance with War Food Orders. It is largely a matter of education, you know. War Food Orders are important means of seeing to it that the available supplies of food get to the right places at the right time. When this is brought home to those affected by the orders, compliance is almost automatic.

ANNOUNCER: It sounds to me like these committees can perform a very valuable service.

OD: They can and they are.

ANNOUNCER: By the way, how widely are they organized?

OD: Here in the west, we have them for almost every major trading area. In (state), we have one in (city), (city), and _____ (AS MANY MORE AS NECESSARY). The committee in (state capital) also serves as a state committee. (Add material on local committee, if available.) Incidentally, _____, I expect that these committees will play a very active part in the coming

(MORE)

OD: (cont.)   campaign on food waste, will go into high gear in the near future.

ANNOUNCER: A campaign on food waste? Do we need one?

OD: Well, give a listen to a few facts on the subject and tell me what you think. About how much food do you buy every year for yourself, _____?

ANNOUNCER: Why.....I don't know exactly -- I never stopped to figure it out -- a couple of pounds a day I should guess. Is that about right?

OD: Not quite, unless you're a very light eater, and you don't look like it to me. If you're an average American civilian, you buy for consumption about 1500 pounds a year -- over 4 pounds per person a day.

ANNOUNCER: I hadn't realized that.

OD: And I'll bet, _____, that you hadn't realized how much of that food you, as an average American civilian, throw away, either

ANNOUNCER: Probably not. How much?

OD: Around three quarters of a pound a day -- about 300 pounds a year --- or between 15 and 25% of what you bought, -- bread, meat, vegetables, fruit -- all going into the garbage can because of incorrect buying, storage, preparation and because of our failure to "lick our platters clean".

ANNOUNCER: Extraordinary, Mr. Holmes!

OD: Elementary, Dr. Watson.

ANNOUNCER: You mean that out of every five meals prepared, entirely in the garbage can?

OD: Not actually, of course, because our food is wa dribbles, here and there, but that's what it a _____, if we could eliminate all the waste occurs in this country, the amount saved would the food armed services are now getting plus a is going to meet our lend lease commitments. eliminate all waste, of course, but we can go that end.

ANNOUNCER: Obviously, a most important thing to do. How about it?

OD: Basically, by bringing the facts to the attent But suppose we leave the details for later bro hear plenty about it soon. _____

ANNOUNCER: Okay, and I'll be looking forward to it. What for us this _____?

OD: Some good news for beef eaters.

ANNOUNCER: That's me. What is it?

OD: Beginning on May 15, the government set aside been reduced from 40 to 35%. War Food Order 7 Federally inspected packers to set aside a ste their choice, good, commercial and utility ste for purchase by the armed forces and war servi in the amount of beef made available for the r

OD: (cont.)   possible by increased marketings of beef cattle. It ought to

show up in your local butcher shop pretty soon.

ANNOUNCER: That's fine.

OD: And if you're a dried prune fancier, you can expect to see more

of those, too. War Food Administration has released an additional

12 million pounds from the 1943 crop for civilian consumption.

More than half the crop is now available for civilians -- the

rest is going to the armed services and lend lease.

ANNOUNCER: That's in line with WFA policy of releasing to civilian consumers

all the food possible in excess of our war requirements, isn't it?

OD: Absolutely. And finally, here's an urgent message of especial

interest to our farm listeners. We need more dry beans for

the war effort. Dry beans are war food -- for our armed forces,

civilians, and our allies. U. S. military and war services

alone will take approximately 19 percent of our 1943 crop. Dry

beans are a fighting food. They come close to meat, eggs, milk,

and cheese as body-builders. Anticipating that some continental

territory may be occupied by our forces by this fall, the 1944

bean crop would become available at a most opportune time. If

the crop is ample, it will go far toward relieving a tight food

situation on those parts of the Continent we occupy. It would

be difficult to produce too many dry beans in 1944 in the United

States.

ANNOUNCER: Well, why are we short now? Wasn't all this thought

of when the 1944 goals were set?

OD: Yes, _____, it was, but when those goals we

       counting on 6 million bags from foreign sourc

       dry beans thus far have been disappointing --

       of the quantity of imports is now only 3 mill

ANNOUNCER: You seem to be pretty good at converting stat

       understandable terms, _____. Tell me, what

       of 3 million bags mean in terms of food?

OD: 3 million bags is enough food for 10 million

       That's how much our imports have fallen off -

       has to be made up through domestic production

ANNOUNCER: But how about the price? Will there be price

OD: There will be price support. War Food Admini

       support the price of dry edible beans by purc

       lots, cleaned and bagged, f.o.b. cars at coun

       at prices for U.S. No. 1 grade beans ranging

       per hundred pounds, according to type.

ANNOUNCER: Farmers, then, are urged to plant more dry be

       methods that will increase yield per acre.

OD: You have it in a nutshell, _____, or should

ANNOUNCER: And there you have it, folks...this week's re

       information. _____, of the State (or area

       bution. War Food Administration will be back

       week at this same time) to give you current r

       on.....Food Fights for Freedom.....At home and

       on America's wartime food program is presente

       _____ farmers and consumers.

FOOD FIGHTS FOR FREEDOM -- AT HOME AND ABROAD
(MRD WEEKLY SCRIPT #10)

Use of this weekly series has been cleared for time by the Office of War
Information over the following radio stations: Z-Bar Network, Montana; KFBC,
Cheyenne, Wyoming; KLO, Ogden, and KDYL, Salt Lake City, Utah; KTAR, Phoenix,
Arizona; Reno and Las Vegas, Nevada; KWG, Stockton, California; KXL, Portland;
KIDO, Boise; and KRLC, Lewiston, Idaho.

NOTE TO STATE AND AREA SUPERVISORS: Suggest you time all scripts in advance.
News section of the script is a good place to make additions or deletions.
War Food Bulletins from this office are a good source of additional news items.

ANNOUNCER:　Good _____, friends. What is your country doing to

　　　　　　manage its food supply?

　　　　　　You'll find out if you listen each week to........

　　　　　　Food Fights for Freedom -- at home and abroad! ...a

　　　　　　presentation of the Office of Distribution, War Food

　　　　　　Administration. Today, we're glad to have _____,

　　　　　　of the (State or Area) office　back here on the other

　　　　　　side of the microphone to give us more news of activities

　　　　　　on the food front. So open up your bag of tricks there,

　　　　　　_____, and lets hear what you've got.

OD:　　　　Well, here's an item on the "Achievement A Award."

ANNOUNCER:　I'll buy it..what else?

OD:　　　　And one on butter....

ANNOUNCER:　I'm still in the market.....

OD:　　　　And one of especial interest to housewives - the foods that

　　　　　　will be available in abundance during June....

ANNOUNCER:　O. K. Let 'er go.

OD:　　　　How are you on flags, _____?

ANNOUNCER: Pretty good. As a matter of fact, I'll have you know
that I was once flag calling champion of _____ county.

OD: Fine. Then you're my man. Tell me, have you ever seen a
large green flag, with a big blue A on it, surrounded with
what looks like a white circle and a star in the corner?

ANNOUNCER: Lets see....large green flag...big blue A....white circle.
star.....No, I don't think I have.

OD: I'm not surprised. That flag is a mark of high achievemen
and you don't see it flying in many places. You'll only
find it in 26 places in the west, incidentally.

ANNOUNCER: This sounds interesting. What does that flag stand for?

OD: It stands for government recognition of an outstanding
job of food production and processing for the war effort.

ANNOUNCER: Are you sure you don't mean the Army-Navy E?

OD: No, I don't mean the E award. As a matter of fact, _____
The Achievement "A" Award was instituted because the
qualifications for receiving the Army-Navy E excluded most
of the food processing plants in the country.

ANNOUNCER: How?

OD: By requiring that a very large percentage of the total
product of the plant go directly into the war effort.

ANNOUNCER: ...and because only about 25% of our total food is going
directly into the war effort - that is, to our soldiers
and our allies - most food plants wouldn't qualify. I see
that.

OD: Exactly - but at the same time, food is most important to our war effort. Soldiers must have weapons to fight - those weapons must be produced - and workers must eat to work. So must we all, for that matter.

ANNOUNCER: In other words, the A Award was set up to honor farmers, management and workers doing an outstanding job of food production and processing.

OD: You have it - if you keep on doing this well, someday I'll let you handle the program all by yourself.

ANNOUNCER: Someday I'll get tired being your straight man, and just take it away. What types of plants are eligible for the award?

(READ FAST)
OD: Canners, Quick Freeze and Cold Packers, Dried Fruit Processors, Vegetable Dehydrators, Citrus Processing Plants...

ANNOUNCER: Take a breath, friend, take a breath....

OD: (FAST) Thank you, Flouring Mills, some kinds of Fish Canners, Manufacturers of Cheddar Cheese, Dry skim milk, Spray process dry whole milk, evaporated and sweetened condensed milk.

ANNOUNCER: Go on, go on, you'll make it!

OD: (Finish with a Rush) Certain kinds of poultry products, and federally inspected meat packing plants selling from 20 to 30 percent of their product to the Federal Government.

ANNOUNCER: Bravo! I knew you could do it.

OD: Thanks. It's easy when you know how.

ANNOUNCER: Well, are you able to continue?

OD: Oh yes, I'm in top form today. Fire away.

ANNOUNCER: All right then. What are the qualifications considered for the the granting of the award?

OD: Well, first of all, the _quantities_ and _quality_ of production in the light of available facilities.

ANNOUNCER: Yes of course, I would think that would be a major factor. And other major factors are ....

OD: Ingenuity and cooperation with the government in developing food production.

ANNOUNCER: Yes....

OD: Cooperation in carrying out the purposes of the various food programs.

ANNOUNCER: That's two.

OD: Effective management, ability to overcome production obstacles, satisfactory management and labor relations, including the avoidance of work stoppages.

ANNOUNCER: Are there more?

OD: A couple. Educational factors, low absentee records, accident prevention , health and sanitation.

ANNOUNCER: Brother, I can see that to qualify for the "A" Award a plant has to be really good. How do you go about finding out?

OD: We make an investigation.

ANNOUNCER: You make an investigation?

OD: If it was in my territory, I would. In other words, the Office of Distribution representative who covers the territory in which the plant is located.

ANNOUNCER: Well, now that we've started, let's carry on through. What happens after you make your investigation?

OD: If the investigation discloses that the plant should be considered

for the award, I send it on to our regional office, where the

material is reviewed by our regional officials who have knowledge

of the whole industry involved.

ANNOUNCER: And if the nomination meets all the qualifications, what then?

OD: It goes to Washington where it's subject to at least two more

reviews.

ANNOUNCER: That's a stiff course to run isn't it?.

OD: Yes it is. It's a series of screening operations, really, to make

sure that only those plants which are fully qualified receive the

award.

ANNOUNCER: Let's presume that they do qualify. What do you do then, just

write them a letter?

OD: Well, we do write them a letter, but that's only a small part

of the rather impressive ceremony which is held for the presentation

of this award.

ANNOUNCER: Oh, there is a ceremony?

OD: Yes, and as I stated, a rather impressive one, usually on Sunday or

in the evening. Generally, all the farmers who help produce the

food and all the people who work in the plant are invited. A high

officer of the Army or Navy makes the presentation of the flag

to officials of the company and a representative of the War Food

Administration presents a handsome pin to representatives of the

employees. And there is music and singing and general celebration.

ANNOUNCER: Do all employees receive pins?

OD: Yes, all those directly concerned with the actual operation do. The presentation is merely a symbolic one. This pin, incidentally, comes on a little card bearing a message from President Roosevelt. "Food", says the President, "is a decisive weapon of war. Victory depends as much on our ability to produce food as as our ability to produce tanks, planes and ships. Our army of producers are fighting an important battle on the food front, working diligently and skilfully to speed our allies on to victory."

               I have here an excerpt from a speech delivered at an "A" Award ceremony in California. It was made by a Captain of the United States Navy and containing some interesting highlights on the part that food is playing in our war effort. I wonder if you'd like to have it?

ANNOUNCER: Yes, I would. (slight pause) Say, this looks interesting. I note he said here "I wonder if the people of this country realize the part they are playing in helping defeat the enemy. They -- and I want to include our farmers -- may sometimes think what the have done and are doing is not of the same degree of importance as the making of specific implements of war. Let me assure you that the products of your efforts are fully as important as the making of planes, tanks and ships and shells."

OD: Yes; and you will notice he went on to say that "in order to insure that every soldier be fed properly, day after day and on time, the army must have on hand at all times 247 days supply of food."

ANNOUNCER: How was that again? Did he say 247 days supply of food?

OD: Yes, he explained it this way, and again I quote. "Our supply lines are long and this means 15 days food supply is always in transit in this country, another 30 days is in transit on the high seas. Still another 65 days supply is on hand at our ports of embarkation."

ANNOUNCER: Let's see, that adds up to 110 days. I would imagine the other 147 is in the storage, transportation and distribution of food after it reaches its destination.

OD: I believe that's correct.

ANNOUNCER: Well tell me, _____, does this award mean very much to the company and the workers who receive it?

OD: You bet it does. Everybody likes to have a good job they've done recognized. And that's what the award is; a recognition of outstanding achievement in the production and processing of food.

ANNOUNCER: Are there any plants in (___state___) which have received this award?

OD: (ANSWER ACCORDING TO SITUATION IN YOUR STATE:

If you have had A Awards, list them.

If you have one coming up, list it.

If neither applies, say "we've had no

A Awards so far in (state), but we are

keeping an eye open for plants that possibly

can qualify")

ANNOUNCER: And now, how about some news from the food front.

OD: Well, here's a paradox for you: although the government, as provided in War Food Order 2 point 1, is going to buy about 50% of the butter produced during next month, there will be more butter available to civilians than during March, when the government didn't buy any.

ANNOUNCER: Oh, I think I can crack that one. The answer would be, I think, that June is a month of very heavy production. Is that right?

OD: Right the first time, in fact. The government tries to buy enough butter during the heavy producing summer months to supply our requirements the year round, so that in times of slim production, the entire amount made will be available to civilians. We are talking, you understand, about creamery production. All farm production goes to civilians.

ANNOUNCER: Still, half of all the creamery butter produced in June will spread a lot of bread. Where does it all go after the government buys it?

OD: About 85% of the butter reserved for government agencies during this year --- representing only 17% of total U. S. annual production of creamery butter --- will go to U. S. Armed forces and other war services.

ANNOUNCER: You mean the Army and Navy and Marines, I suppose?

OD: Yes, and the Coast Guard, Veteran's Administration and the War Shipping Administration.

ANNOUNCER: That leaves 15% unaccounted for. Let's see -- that would be about 3% of our total production.

OD: That other 15% of butter set aside for government use will be purchased by the War Food Administration to complete the lend-lease, territorial and Red Cross allocations for the year.

ANNOUNCER: When will the government stop buying butter?

OD: Of course, the only real answer I can give you on that one is -- when we have enough butter to supply our war needs. But last year, the government bought no butter from October 1 through March, 1944. It ought to be about the same this time.

ANNOUNCER: Now, how about a note to our family buyer listeners - what foods
              may they expect to see on the market in abundance during June?

OD: During June, there will be plentiful supply in most parts of
              the country of: Eggs.

ANNOUNCER: Eggs.

OD: White potatoes.

ANNOUNCER: The new crop of White potatoes.

OD: Canned peas, and canned green and wax beans.

ANNOUNCER: What about fresh vegetables?

OD: There should be plenty of peas, lettuce, carrots, beets and
              artichokes.

ANNOUNCER: And do you, sir, have a final thought for the week?

OD: I do, sir. You may chew on this until we meet again. From
              October to the First of March, WFA bought enough eggs and egg
              powder to support the market and to supply war needs to make
              an omelet one mile long, one mile wide, and 40 feet high. That's
              before the omelet falls, of course.

ANNOUNCER: Well, if you don't mind _____, I'll wait for the fall
              before I start to chew on that omelet. I've got enough hot air
              in me now.

OD: As who, my friend, has not?

ANNOUNCER: That does it, chum. This weeks report on warfood information is
              in the bag. _____ , of the State (or Area) office of
              Distribution, War Food Administration, will be back with us
              next week at this time (or soon) to give us more current news
              and information on....Food Fights For Freedom....at home and
              abroad. This program on America's wartime food program is
              presented especially for _____ listeners.

WAR FOOD ADMINISTRATION   Approx. 15 minutes
Office of Distribution   )   May 19, 1944
821 Market Street, Room 700   State and Area Supervisors
San Francisco 3, California   Can Cut to fit allotted time.
rye
42.2

FOOD FIGHTS FOR FREEDOM -- AT HOME AND ABROAD
(WRD WEEKLY SCRIPT #11)

Use of this weekly series has been cleared for time by the Office of War Information over the following radio stations: Z-Bar Network, Montana; KFBC, Cheyenne,
Wyoming; KLO, Ogden, and KDYL, Salt Lake City, Utah; KTAR, Phoenix, Arizona; Reno
and Las Vegas, Nevada; KWG, Stockton, California; KXL, Portland; KIDO, Boise; and
KRLC, Lewiston, Idaho.

NOTE TO STATE AND AREA SUPERVISORS: Suggest you time all scripts in advance. News
section of the script is a good place to make additions or deletions. War Food
Bulletins from this office are a good source of additional news items.

ANNOUNCER: Good _____, friends. What is your country doing to manage

                its food supply? What can you do to help? You'll find out if you

                listen each week to.......

                Food Fights For Freedom -- at home and abroad!.....a presentation

                of the Office of Distribution, War Food Administration. Today, we're

                glad to have _____, of the (state or area) office back

                here on the other side of the microphone to give us more news of

                activities on the food front. What's cooking on the front and back

                burners today, _____?

OD: The government has taken further action to make more meat available

                to the folks here at home, especially in our smaller towns and

                rural communtiies. How's that for a starter?

ANNOUNCER: That's good enough for the left front burner with the gas full on.

                What else?

OD: A new and simplified government egg buying program has been

                instituted, which ought to help out our egg producers.

ANNOUNCER: There's room for that on our verbal stove, too.

OD: And finally I want to tell you a little bit about an Office of Distribution supported program to can foods for school lunches and child feeding centers that many of our listeners will be able to help with.

ANNOUNCER: I see we have a full fifteen minutes ahead. Now how about item number one, this business of more meat to be available for consumers that you mentioned. Is that to be brought about through a change in a War Food Order?

OD: Yes,_____, it is, in a sense. You've heard of War Food Order number seventy-five, haven't you?

ANNOUNCER: I'm sure I have. Thats the War Food Order which has to do with the slaughter and allocation of our meat supply, isn't it?

OD: Precisely. Well, all of War Food Order 75's restrictions on farm slaughter of livestock and delivery of meat to customers were lifted as of May 25.

ANNOUNCER: Let's see if I've got you straight. You say that all restrcitions on farm slaughter of livestock and delivery to off-farm customers have been lifted. Just how were these things limited before that?

OD: Farmers have been required to obtain a permit from the Office of Distribution through County Triple A Committees to slaughter and deliver livestock to off-farm customers. What they were allowed to slaughter was largely determined by what they had killed during the base period of 1941. This meant that unless some unusual justification existed, a farmer who hadn't killed any livestock during the base period was stuck. These restrictions, of course, were necessary at the time they were imposed and for a period after that because our armed forces and our allies had to have a lot of meat — they still do, of course – but other factors in the picture have changed very considerably.

-3-

ANNOUNCER: Well, _____, if my memory serves correctly, weren't restictions on this type of killing and sale of hogs lifted sometime ago?

OD: Yes, _____, that's right, but they still applied to other types of livestock until amendment 15 to War Food Order 75 was issued, taking effect May 25, as I said.

ANNOUNCER: I'd be interested to have you explain in more detail just what you meant when you said that the picture had changed.

OD: That's a pretty big assignment, _____, and we only have 15 minutes. I might be able to do it in a couple of hours....

ANNOUNCER: Well put, friend. So let me phrase my question this way: What are the most important factors bringing about this change to permit farmers to slaughter and sell all types of livestock to non farm customers?

OD: The most important reasons would shape out about like this: First, cattle on the range that is, on pasture, have been steadily increasing in number during the last few years. Second, feed lot operations have sharply declined during the past year.

ANNOUNCER: I know that. Partly, I believe, the price situation, partly lack of labor and partly the lack of feed.

OD: Right. And that leads me on to the next reason - the supply of feed of all kinds both range pasture and small grains and concentrates is not large enough to feed the number of cattle on the range. Fourth, the large packing houses are experiencing acute difficulties with lack of labor.

ANNOUNCER: Would it then be accurate to sum it up this way; there are too many cattle on the range for the feed supply, and a good deal of this excess cannot be marketed through major packers because of various factors, one important one being the lack of labor.

OD: That's about it — naturally,_____, the more meat animals we have on the range and in the feed lots, the better IF there is enough feed. But there isn't. The weather has not been too favorable and crops are either below normal or very late. Another factor has been the diversion of wheat, barley and other small grains to direct industrial use — the manufacture of industrial alcohol for explosives and rubber, for example.

ANNOUNCER: So, it becomes necessary to facilitate movement of heavy supplies of livestock now on farms into consumer channels.

OD: One way to do that is to permit farmers to slaughter and deliver to off-farm customers without restriction as far as the WFA is concerned. Of course, farmers must still pick up ration points for those cuts which are still rationed.

ANNOUNCER: One more question on this: Why will this have primary effect on small towns and rural communities?

OD: Most larger cities depend on large packers for the major part of their meat supplies, but during the war many smaller communities draw a large portion of their meat direct from the farmer himself.

ANNOUNCER: I see. You expect this new outlet to help relieve the current overstocking of the range, and to bring the number of cattle on the hoof more in line with our feed supplies.

OD: That's right.

ANNOUNCER: All right. Now what about the egg purchase program?

OD: It isn't a new program_____, since the War Food Administration has been buying eggs in carlot quantities right along, but it embodies some changes which should make it easier for producers to offer their eggs and contains one very important new feature for thi type of purchase.

ANNOUNCER: Just how does a purchase program of this type work, _____?

OD: First of all, our regional office issued a purchase announcement,
             which specifies the quantity of eggs which may be offered, the
             grades which will be bought, how they must be packed, what prices
             will be paid, and so forth.

ANNOUNCER: After a producer, or egg assembler who wishes to sell to the
             government receives one of these announcements, what does he do?

OD: He wires or writes to our Regional Office Dairy and Poultry
             Division giving all the information required by the purchase
             announcement.

ANNOUNCER: And if his offer is accepted?

OD: He will receive a notice of acceptance from Office of Distribution,
             and shortly thereafter, shipping instructions. The eggs must be
             inspected and graded by federal graders, of course, to make sure
             they meet the specifications. After the eggs are shipped the
             vendor submits a voucher and receives payment in the form of
             a government check. That's not all there is to it, but that is
             'a rough outline of how it works.

ANNOUNCER: That seems simple enough. Now how about the changes in the new
             purchase announcement.

OD: First of all, consumer grades have been eliminated for these
             eggs, although government procurement grades are still used.
             This will simplify the vendor's grading problems

ANNOUNCER: What else?

OD: The prices to be paid for eggs are the same through out the region. The Freight Differentials, which meant different prices for the same eggs in different places, have been eliminated. This is also a simplification.

ANNOUNCER: I see that.

OD: And the most important thing is the specification in the contract that the vendor or assembler must have paid the producer not less than 27¢ a dozen for the eggs on a field run - or losse - basis.

ANNOUNCER: That's assurance that the producers will receive a fair price for his eggs.

OD: That's right.

ANNOUNCER: _____, where may an interested producer or egg assembler obtain copies of this purchase announcement?

OD: I can supply him with one. Our office is located at __(address)__. Or he can get one from our Regional Office - Dairy and Poultry Division, Office of Distribution, War Food Administration, Western Region, 821 Market Street, Room 700, San Francisco 3, California.

ANNOUNCER: And what's the title of this announcement?

OD: Announcement A-W-D-1, Western Region, Purchase of Fresh Shell Eggs.

ANNOUNCER: Let me repeat that - Announcement A-W-D-1, Western Region, Purchase of Fresh Shell Eggs.

OD: Do we have enough time left for a little dope on the Community School Lunch Canning Program, _____?

ANNOUNCER: I think so, fire away.

OD: You're familiar, arn't you _____, with the work of the Community Canning Centers.

ANNOUNCER: I should say I am. There's one out here at _____. Victory Gardeners can get together, purchase cans at a wholesale price, and use the facilities of the canning center, which include pressure cookers, sealers, etc., to put up their garden produce under professional supervision. We make use of it in my family.

OD: This program is built around the idea of putting together these canning facilities with fresh fruits and vegetables the War Food Administration will buy to support price and relieve markets this summer, to supply school lunch programs with food for the fall and winter.

ANNOUNCER: That's a whale of a good idea. How does it work?

OD: This program begins, as most do, with a group of people getting together - in this case, a group of eligible school lunch or child care-center sponsoring agencies which are near a community canning center, or have other proper facilities available.

ANNOUNCER: Why must there be a group? Why can't just one school or child-care-center sponsoring agency take on the program?

OD: It will mostly be a group because the quantity of the commodities available will usually be too great for any one school to handle. In general, they will come in car or half car lots, but exceptions are entirely possible. The program is very flexible this way.

ANNOUNCER: O.K. go on. I suppose the next thing this group would do would
be to sign agreements with the Office of Distribution. Right?

OD: Right. Then they allocate the distribution of the commodity, and
work out a plan for the necessary labor.

ANNOUNCER: Then when the commodities arrive, they get together and can it
in the Community Canning Center. Who pays for the cans?

OD: The Office of Distribution will reimburse the sponsoring agencies
in an amount approximately equal to the cost of the cans.

ANNOUNCER: Then it won't cost them anything at all?

OD: Well, let me put it this way. If all the labor necessary is
volunteered, and if all the trucking necessary for the unloading
transport and distribution is provided free by public spirited
members of the group or by school officials, and if the cans can
be had at a reasonable price - it wouldn't cost anything.

ANNOUNCER: In other words, it depends on the amount of cooperation. That's
fair enough. The processed food then goes to the schools and
child welfare centers where it is used in the school or child care
center lunch program, does it not?

OD: It does. And as you can see, the program has done a lot of people
good.

ANNOUNCER: Yes, I can see that. The producer is assisted through price
support and market relief, the sponsors get a lot of practice
in the elements of successful canning and the satisfaction
of community cooperation, and our youngsters get food at school,

OD: One variation of the type of program we've been talking about might be mentioned - sponsoring groups can have the canning done for them at properly equipped custom canneries, if they wish,

ANNOUNCER: Your office can supply fuller information, I suppose, _____.

OD: You bet. The address again is ___(address)___ . Interested people might write.

ANNOUNCER: I hope they will. This program sounds like a very good thing. _____, our time is about up. Have you a final thought?

OD: Just a final reminder, _____, that onions are back on the market in plentiful supply. All those people who hunted for them in vain during the last few months can now get all they want. The early crop is in. The variety of onions coming on the market now doesnot store well and should be used as you buy them.

ANNOUNCER: Here's our chance to make all those onion dishes we thought about when they weren't available. Thanks for the tip, _____. (AND SO INTO CONVENTIONAL CLOSE).

Lightning Source UK Ltd.
Milton Keynes UK
UKHW012330061118
331891UK00010B/972/P